T0111788

UNAGI

CENTRAL PERK

Smelly Cat

We Were on a BREAK!

TRANSPONSTERS INC.

Pivot

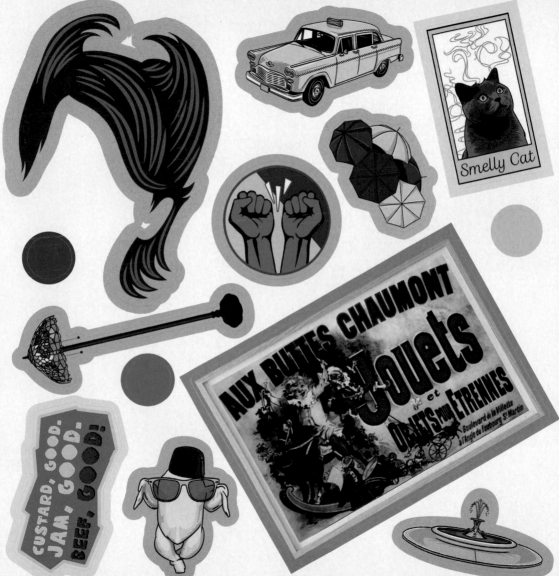

Smelly Cat

CUSTARD, GOOD.
JAM, GOOD.
BEEF, GOOD!

AUX BUTTES CHAUMONT
Jouets
et
OBJETS POUR ÉTRENNES
Boulevard de la Villette
à l'Angle du Faubourg St Martin

MOO POINT

Pivot

I'll be THERE FOR You

Fire Beats Everything

MARCEL

SPUDNIK

New York City

MARCEL

I Know!

SPUDNIK

New York City

CENTRAL PERK

UNAGI

I Know!

Fire Beats

MUSEUM OF

PREHISTORIC HISTORY

Seven!

CENTRAL PERK

AUX BUTTES CHAUMONT
Jouets
OBJETS pour ETRENNES

NEW YORK CITY

DOESN'T SHARE FOOD

Smelly Cat

HOW YOU DOIN'?

TRANSPONSTERS INC.

NEW YORK CITY

I'll be THERE FOR you

Pivot

I Know!

UNAGI

MARCEL

Fire Beats Everything

CUSTARD. GOOD. JAM. GOOD. BEEF. GOOD!

MUSEUM OF PREHISTORIC HISTORY

MOO POINT

New York City

Seven!

DOESN'T SHARE
FOOD

MUSEUM OF

PREHISTORIC
HISTORY

CENTRAL
PERK

**MOO
POINT**

I'll be
THERE for
you

AUX BUTTES CHAUMONT
Jouets
et
OBJETS POUR ETRENNES

CUSTARD, GOOD.
JAM, GOOD.
BEEF, GOOD!

Seven!

HOW YOU DOIN'?

Floor

Cheesecake

DOESN'T SHARE **FOOD**

Fire Beats
Everything

I know!

MOO POINT

I'll be THERE FOR you

New York City

Seven!

MUSEUM OF

PREHISTORIC HISTORY

I'll be THERE for you

NEW YORK CITY

Floor
Cheesecake

Pivor

DOESN'T SHARE FOOD

SPUDNIK

I know!

CENTRAL PERK

MOO POINT

MUSEUM OF

PREHISTORIC HISTORY

AUX BUTTES CHAUMONT
Jouets et OBJETS POUR ETRENNES

Seven!

HOW You DOIN'?

Pivot

MOO POINT

NEW YORK CITY

Floor

Cheesecake

Smelly Cat

WE WERE ON A BREAK!

New York City